Journeying
with the Magi

Journeying
with the Magi

An Advent Course
in the Celtic Tradition

Keith Duke

kevin mayhew

First published in 2004 by
KEVIN MAYHEW LTD
Buxhall, Stowmarket, Suffolk, IP14 3BW
info@kevinmayhewltd.com

9 8 7 6 5 4 3 2

ISBN 978 1 84417 278 8
Catalogue No. 1500714

Cover design by Sara-Jane Came
Edited by Marian Reid
Typesetting by Richard Weaver

Printed and bound in Great Britain

CONTENTS

ACKNOWLEDGEMENTS

My thanks are due to many, but especially to the Celtic Spirituality Group here in North Lincolnshire who first gave me the opportunity to lead a session on the Journey of the Magi as part of their Advent Course in 2002; it was from this session that this course developed.

My special thanks to Val Whitaker who has read through all of this material at its different stages of development and always made constructive suggestions for its improvement; and to Anna Leggett at Kevin Mayhew Publishers for her support and co-operation.

My thanks also to the following for permission to use their copyright material: Kathy Galloway for the extract from 'Cross-Border Peace Talks', from her poetry collection *Pushing the Boat Out*; Neil Douglas-Klotz for his thoughtful reading of the Aramaic Lord's Prayer in *Prayers of the Cosmos*, and of the sayings of Jesus in *The Hidden Gospel – the Spiritual Message of the Aramaic Jesus*; Glennie Kindred for her thoughts on Samhain from her excellent book *Sacred Celebrations*; Michael Mitton for the quotation from his challenging book *Restoring the Woven Cord*; and, finally, Robert van de Weyer for his poem 'Brendan's prayer on the mountain' from *Celtic Fire*.

INTRODUCTION

One Saturday evening I was driving my teenage daughter and her friends to a birthday disco and they were chatting away in the back of the car. At the roundabout adjacent to the hall the road was blocked. Clearly there was some sort of major incident: police cars, blue-flashing lights, uniformed officers everywhere – except that they were all standing still. A slow convoy approached along the dual carriageway from Lincolnshire, and I reckoned it was some kind of huge engineering project, a plane fuselage, maybe, on a low-loader, snaking its way through the countryside with a safety escort. I was wrong: it was a group of Travellers being escorted from Lincolnshire through north Nottinghamshire, presumably into South Yorkshire, with all surrounding roads blocked off, and no possibility of their deviating from the planned route.

I watched the long line of vans, lorries and caravans pass with their police escort and wondered what was going on. What had these people done? Had their behaviour been so terrible that they were being expelled from Lincolnshire and were being taken to a 'soft' county where they would be more accepted? Perhaps some of them had been arrested and locked up, and, if so, was this justified, and what would happen to them? I found myself thinking about what kind of mind-set triggered a chain of events like this, and what prejudices existed in high places. I thought about the travellers and how they might be feeling. Where did *my* sympathies lie? What assumptions was I making about the police? What assumptions was I making about the travellers? What assumptions were the police and the travellers making? Could their differing points of view be reconciled? Does it matter?

In 1999, Channel 4 broadcast a series of six programmes entitled *This is Modern Art*, presented by Matthew Collings. I love all this modern art stuff. When I'm in London, I wander the Tate Modern, absorbing its vibrant energies of creativity, colour, challenge, thoughtfulness, shape, anarchy, humour, disbelief and abandoned journeying. At first, I found Matthew Collings irritating. I was hoping for a nice cosy journey through key contemporary art that would help me understand a little more of what it was all about and all I seemed to get were unhelpful, fragmented statements and foolish questions! Modern Art: why do we like it? What is it, anyway? What's he doing it for? I wonder what I'm going to say? He made that up. So what? What's happening? and the maddening: Does it matter?

'Of course it does,' I almost scream, 'otherwise I wouldn't be watching!' I watched the whole series, because Matthew Collings took me on a journey where I learned well because I had to work at learning. I had to make my own response; had to think and respond in ways that gave me ownership of my learning. I wasn't told what to think, and I wasn't irritated for long.

These two tales (dare I say parables?) present two possible models of spiritual journeying. The first is carefully planned and effective but has all other avenues of enquiry, belief and understanding closed off; the second is much more open-ended and, by asking questions rather than giving answers, empowers everyone to learn and journey from where they are. In this Advent course I aim to work with the second model. I aim to present information and ask questions – lots of questions. Some of these questions will seem mundane, simple-minded or even irritating, but, hopefully, along with those that are OK, they will open up discussion about what we believe, why we believe it, and why we can and should believe different things on the evidence that is available (and on our own experience) rather than because a tradition or individual says we must. Hopefully, we will often ask the question 'Does it matter?', and come to the conclusion that sometimes it does, and sometimes it doesn't. So much modern art, whatever the medium, does demand we come to a state of under-standing and knowing for ourselves; I believe the same applies for our spiritual journey with God and Jesus and, in this case, the Magi.

Keith Duke, May 2004

NOTES FOR LEADERS

A course in five parts is an excellent opportunity for five different people (or five pairs of people) to lead a session each, and it's also an opportunity for the usual organiser to take a back seat. So if you're the priest, vicar, worship leader, or whoever, this is your time to be 'done unto' – make the most of it; it probably doesn't happen that often!

The Leader's Role
The role of the leader is simply to help each session move along within the allotted time. This will happen more easily if you:

- know the material well by thoroughly reading the course, or at least your part of it;
- are aware of the resources needed and have them readily available;
- make sure the group knows exactly what to do and how much time they have to do it in;
- provide opportunities for everyone to contribute;
- gently hold back those who tend to dominate the discussion, whoever they are!
- don't expect to be perfect; nobody is, however good they might seem!

Requirements for Each Session
- a copy of this booklet for each person involved;
- a good supply of paper, pens, pencils, etc., so participants can make notes;
- a flipchart or large sheets of paper and large pens to record the points shared in the feedback sessions;
- song words and a musician (with instrument?) if you intend to sing;
- refreshments with someone else designated to prepare and serve them.

Also Needed

- bread and wine in suitable containers if you intend to share the Eucharist at the end of the session;
- CD and/or tape player with suitably gentle instrumental music;
- visual materials: perhaps some gold, frankincense and myrrh; anything that will help illustrate the content of the course;
- candles, matches, incense, textiles, stones, etc., that will help create a prayerful space, especially if you wish to include a time of open prayer;
- space and comfort: if possible, use a space which will not be overcrowded and which has comfortable chairs.

The Sessions

The five sessions of the course should be completed before Christmas, preferably undertaken over a five-week period starting in November. They need be of no specified fixed length of time, as each will vary according to the experience of the group and how willing the participants are to discuss issues in depth, but I would suggest that perhaps a half-hour be given to each discussion and feedback section, and a half-hour be given over to worship, silences and other activities. If half-day sessions are held, then each discussion and feedback session could be longer, the questions approached in more depth, and the silences extended to allow more personal reflection. Silence is an important part of the course, but it can be difficult to manage, especially with groups who are not used to it. It's often helpful to have a two- or three-minute track of very gentle instrumental music playing in the background to aid reflection and mark the passage of time, and there is an instrumental track on both *Sacred Weave* and *Sacred Pathway* (see Suitable Songs and Recordings at the back of this book).

The Sources

The sources given in the following pages have been grouped together at the beginning, partly to avoid the need to reprint them in different sessions, and also to allow them to be read as a whole by everyone before the first session. The structure of each session is the same, but may be adjusted according to circumstances. Opportunities are given for welcome and feedback at each session, though these should be kept brief. The periods of silence are important as they allow us to reflect more deeply on the discussion, and organise or store our thoughts before we move on. The first 'Group or Individual Exploration' of each session is designed to look at a part of the Magi story and its meaning, and the second, to look at ways of applying this learning. The format of breaking into small groups and then feeding back to the whole group allows us to consider a greater variety of views than when working as a whole, as well as allowing those of us who are more nervous to contribute. How you organise this will depend on the total number of participants.

Part way through each session there is an 'Other Activity' slot for a song, poem, section of video, drama or visual material. Please use this time creatively; sing, or have one of the group share a song or poem or painting that is relevant to the session.

The Opening and Closing Worship

These sections are a vital part of each session. I also suggest there might be a sharing of bread and wine at the end of the final session. You may also wish to include open prayer in any or all of the sessions (we usually do), though I have not specified prayer time within the sessions as many groups run an Advent course in addition to their regular prayer events. Please use the liturgies in this booklet. They may be unfamiliar at first, as they have been created in the Celtic tradition, but their value lies in their simplicity and challenge. When blessing and sharing Communion, your church tradition may require that you have a priest to do this. But you are free to choose a leader from the group to pass bread and wine around the circle, each person adding a blessing of their own to that already given by the leader. Also feel free to use any of these liturgies elsewhere. The songs and recordings have been suggested because they reflect the content of the course and are very accessible. Should you have difficulty getting hold of them, you can contact the Sales Department at Kevin Mayhew Publishers, or myself, and we will be happy to assist you.

Finally, please encourage everyone to be creative. There are a wealth of poets, composers, songwriters, painters, photographers, sculptors, dancers, actors, playwrights and performance artists out there who create wondrous things. I feel strongly that we desperately need new hymns, songs, poems, prayers, sketches and images that reflect the new understandings we have of the birth of Jesus and the significance of the Magi's visit. Go for it, and share what they create with us!

Journeying

To get to that place,
you have to go
(or be pushed out)
beyond the borders,
to where it is lonely, fearful, threatening, unknown.
Only after you have wandered for a long time
in the dark,
do you begin to bump into others,
also branded, exiled,
border-crossers,
and find you walk on common ground.

from 'Cross-border peace talks' in
Pushing the Boat Out by Kathy Galloway

'Ear Cleaning'

The following quotations are from *Ear Cleaning*, a book by the Canadian composer and educationalist R. Murray Schafer. What he says here about music and sound might also apply to many aspects of our spiritual journey. Simply change the word 'music' or 'sound' to 'prayer', 'healing', 'the gospel', 'pain', or any other aspect of our life experience, and see what happens!

One learns practically nothing about the actual functioning of music by sitting in mute surrender before it . . . one learns about sound only by making sound, about music only by making music.

Improvisory and creative abilities – atrophied through years of disuse – are also rediscovered, and the student learns something very practical about the size and shape of things musical.

SOURCES

All the Gospel references below include both chapter and verse to enable those taking part to use other translations during the course, or to look up the references at their leisure. It is usual practice within our Celtic group to only give the chapter as a reference as this encourages those who follow them up to read the whole chapter and see the quotation in its full context.

A. MATTHEW 2:1-18

After Jesus was born in Bethlehem in Judea, during the time of King Herod, Magi from the east came to Jerusalem and asked, 'Where is the one who has been born king of the Jews? We saw his star in the east and have come to worship him.'

When King Herod heard this he was disturbed, and all Jerusalem with him. When he had called together all the people's chief priests and teachers of the law, he asked them where the Christ was to be born. 'In Bethlehem in Judea,' they replied, 'for this is what the prophet has written:

'"But you, Bethlehem, in the land of Judah, are by no means least among the rulers of Judah; for out of you will come a ruler who will be the shepherd of my people Israel."'

Then Herod called the Magi secretly and found out from them the exact time the star had appeared. He sent them to Bethlehem and said, 'Go and make a careful search for the child. As soon as you find him, report to me, so that I too may go and worship him.'

After they had heard the king, they went on their way, and the star they had seen in the east went ahead of them until it stopped over the place where the child was. When they saw the star, they were overjoyed. On coming to the house, they saw the child with his mother Mary, and they bowed down and worshipped him. Then they opened their treasures and presented him with gifts of gold and of incense and of myrrh. And having been warned in a dream not to go back to Herod, they returned to their country by another route.

When they had gone, an angel of the Lord appeared to Joseph in a dream. 'Get up,' he said, 'take the child and his mother and escape to Egypt. Stay there until I tell you, for Herod is going to search for the child to kill him.' So he got up, took the child and his mother during the night and left for Egypt, where he stayed until the death of Herod. And so was fulfilled what the Lord had said through the prophet: 'Out of Egypt I called my son.' When Herod realised that he had been outwitted by the Magi, he was furious, and he gave orders to kill all the boys in Bethlehem and its vicinity who were two years old and under, in accordance with the time he had learned from the Magi. Then what was said through the prophet Jeremiah was fulfilled:

> 'A voice is heard in Ramah,
> weeping and great mourning,
> Rachel weeping for her children
> and refusing to be comforted,
> because they are no more.'

B. THE GOSPEL OF JOSEPH THE PRIEST 3:1-10; 4:1-3

This Gospel is ascribed to Joseph the High Priest (also known as Caiaphas) and was used by the Eastern churches in the second century. This Gospel was declared unsound in the sixteenth century, purely, it seems, because it was read by an 'undesirable sect' – the Nestorians. As the source used was originally published in 1820, I felt it necessary to update the language. I have, however, kept the phrase 'wise men', though the original is still likely to have been magios.

When the Jesus was born in Bethlehem, a city in Judea, at the time when Herod was King, wise men came from the East to Jerusalem, and, according to the prophecy of Zoradascht [Zoroaster], brought with them offerings, namely gold, frankincense and myrrh, and worshipped him while offering their gifts. Then Mary took one of his swaddling clothes in which the infant was wrapped, and gave it to them instead of a blessing, which they accepted from her as a very suitable present. At the same time there appeared to them an angel in the form of the star, which had been the guide for their journey, the light of which they followed until they returned to their own country. On their return their rulers came and asked what they had seen and done, what sort of journey they had experienced, and what company they had on the road. Instead of answering, they produced the swaddling cloth, which Mary had given them, and on account of which they had kept a feast. Then, according to the custom of their country, they made a fire, and worshipped it, and, when they threw the swaddling cloth into it, the fire took it and held it. When the fire was put out, they took out the swaddling cloth untouched by the fire and began to kiss it, and put it on their heads and eyes, saying, 'It is true, and surprising, that the fire could not burn it.' Then they took it, and with the greatest respect laid it among their treasures. Now Herod, perceiving that the wise men would not return to him, called together the priests and the wise men and said, 'Tell me, where the Christ should be born?' They replied, 'In Bethlehem in Judea.' He then began to contrive the death of Jesus, but an angel appeared to Joseph in his sleep, and said, 'Get up, take the child and his mother, and go to Egypt as soon as the cock crows.' So he got up, and went.

C. THE GOSPEL OF JAMES 15:1-11; 16:1, 2

This Gospel was written in Hebrew, and is ascribed to James, the 'brother and cousin' of Jesus, who later became the first Bishop of Jerusalem. It was widely read in the early Church, and is still in use in some eastern churches. This Gospel was declared unsound essentially because it portrays Joseph as an old man and a widower with a family that conflicted with the official doctrine that Joseph was also a virgin. As the source used was originally published in 1820, I felt it necessary to update the language. I have, however, kept the phrase 'wise men', though the original is still likely to have been magios.

Joseph was preparing to go away because there was great disorder in Bethlehem caused by the visit of some wise men from the east, who asked, 'Where is the king of the Jews to be born, for we have seen his star in the east, and have come to worship him?' When Herod heard this, he was very troubled, and sent messengers to the wise men and to the priests, and brought them to the town-hall, and asked, 'Where is it written about Christ the King; where should he be born?' They said to him, 'In Bethlehem, in Judea, for it is written: "Bethlehem, in the land of Judah, out of you shall come a ruler, who shall rule my people Israel."' He sent away the chief priests and asked the wise men, 'What sign did you see that told you the king has been born?' They answered him, 'We saw an extraordinary large star shining in the heavens that so outshone all the other stars, they became invisible, and we knew that a great king had been born in Israel; therefore, we have come to worship him.' Herod then said, 'Go and make further enquiries, and, if you find the child, come back and tell me so I can worship him also.' So the wise men set off, and the star they had seen in the east went before them until it stood over the cave where the young child was with Mary, his mother. Then they offered him gold, frankincense and myrrh from their treasures. Then, being warned by an angel in a dream that they should not return to Herod, they went to their own country another way. Then Herod, realising that he had been deceived by the wise men, became very angry and commanded some of his men to kill all the children in Bethlehem who were two years old and under. But Mary, hearing that the children were to be killed, became afraid and took the child Jesus, wrapped him in his swaddling clothes and put him in an ox-manger because there was no room for them in the inn.

D. WORDS OF JESUS

Matthew 6:24

No one can serve two masters. Either he will hate the one and love the other, or he will be devoted to the one and despise the other. You cannot serve both God and Money.

Matthew 6:24 – from the Aramaic

You cannot plough two rows at once, cultivate two minds in meditation or follow two different rays back to Unity [God]. You will either turn away from one light, like the moon waning, and shine from the depths towards the other, radiant like the sun . . . you cannot work for Unity without being unified. You cannot cultivate the depths and simultaneously pile things up on the surface of life.

Matthew 16:25-26

For whoever wants to save his life will lose it, but whoever loses his life for me will find it. What good will it be for a man if he gains the whole world, yet forfeits his soul?

Matthew 16:26 – from the Aramaic

For how does it help a human being to know diversity and abundance outside but lack inner life?

Matthew 6:19-21

Do not store up for yourselves treasures on earth, where moth and rust destroy, and where thieves break in and steal. But store up for yourselves treasures in heaven . . . For where your treasure is, there your heart will be also.

Mark 10:17-25

As Jesus started on his way, a man ran up to him and fell on his knees before him. 'Good teacher,' he asked, 'what must I do to inherit eternal life?'

'Why do you call me good?' Jesus answered. 'No one is good – except God alone. You know the commandments: "Do not murder, do not commit adultery, do not steal, do not give false testimony, do not defraud, honour your father and mother."'

'Teacher,' he declared, 'all these I have kept since I was a boy.'

Jesus looked at him and loved him. 'One thing you lack,' he said. 'Go, sell everything you have and give to the poor, and you will have treasure in heaven. Then come, follow me.'

At this the man's face fell. He went away sad, because he had great wealth.

Jesus looked around and said to his disciples, 'How hard it is for the rich to enter the kingdom of God!'

The disciples were amazed at his words. But Jesus said again, 'Children, how hard it is to enter the kingdom of God! It is easier for a camel to go through the eye of a needle than for a rich man to enter the kingdom of God.'

E. PRAYER

Matthew 6:9-13

[Jesus said,] 'This, then, is how you should pray:
"Our Father in heaven,
hallowed be your name,
your kingdom come,
your will be done
on earth as it is in heaven.
Give us today our daily bread.
Forgive us our debts,
as we also have forgiven our debtors.
And lead us not into temptation, but deliver us from the evil one."'

Matthew 6:9-13 – from the Aramaic

O source of all, Mother-Father of Creation, in peace your name resides within us.
Create your reign of unity now, as we find your love in ours,
let heaven and nature form a new creation.
Grant what we need each day in bread and insight.
Loose the cords of mistakes binding us, as we release the strands we hold of others' guilt.
Don't let surface things delude us, but free us from what holds us back from our true purpose.
From you is born each fertile function: ideals, energy, harmony, and from age to age it renews.

Truly, power to these statements.
May they be the ground from which all my actions grow, sealed in
   trust and faith.

> Many of these Celtic prayers are beautifully and poetically written
> and are designed to stir the soul and touch the heart. With the
> Celtic love for creation, many connect with the seasons and with
> all the various aspects of life in God's created order. Celtic Chris-
> tians found it as natural to pray during the milking of the cow as
> they did in church. In fact it was vital to feel at ease in praying
> while doing such mundane things as milking your cow, because
> if you could not do that your spiritual and earthly worlds were
> becoming far too separate. Thus there are prayers for getting up
> in the morning, for washing and dressing, for working, for resting,
> for meeting friends, for eating, for tidying the house, for un-
> dressing, for going to bed.
>
> *Restoring the Woven Cord*, Michael Mitton

Many sources suggest, and I believe, that Celtic spirituality effec-
tively reveals all work as prayer and all prayer as work. The implica-
tions of this are enormous. In one sense, therefore, we are constantly
at prayer through everything we think and do, and also constantly
in a state of communication with God. Consequently, the intention
we hold within our thoughts and actions is of crucial importance to
the nature of the healing response we, and others, receive.

F. JESUS GIVES INSTRUCTIONS TO HIS DISCIPLES

Jesus called his twelve disciples together and sent them out with the
following instructions: 'Go and preach: "The kingdom of heaven is
near." Heal the sick, bring the dead back to life, heal those who suffer
from dreaded skin diseases and drive out demons. You have received
without paying, so give without being paid. Do not carry any gold,
silver or copper money in your pockets; do not carry a beggar's bag
for the journey or an extra shirt or shoes or a stick. A worker should
be given what he needs.'

Adapted from Matthew 10:5-10

G. WE THREE KINGS – A VICTORIAN VIEW

We three kings of Orient are,
bearing gifts we traverse afar;
field and fountain, moor and mountain,
following yonder star.

O star of wonder, star of night,
star with royal beauty bright,
westward leading, still proceeding,
guide us to thy perfect light.

Born a king on Bethlehem plain,
gold I bring, to crown him again,
king for ever, ceasing never,
over us all to reign:

O star of wonder, etc.

Frankincense to offer have I,
incense owns a deity nigh,
prayer and praising, all men raising,
worship him, God most high.

O star of wonder, etc.

Myrrh is mine, its bitter perfume
breathes a life of gathering gloom;
sorrowing, sighing, bleeding, dying,
sealed in a stone-cold tomb.

O star of wonder, etc.

Glorious now, behold him arise,
King, and God, and sacrifice;
heaven sings alleluia,
alleluia the earth replies.

O star of wonder, etc.

John Henry Hopkins (1820–91)

H. THE MAGI

Matthew calls the second group of Jesus' visitors *Magoi*, which refers to those who were very learned; possibly priests, possibly also magicians. From Matthew's account, they certainly had knowledge of what we would call astronomy and astrology (not clearly distinguishable at that time) and we know there were more than two as he refers to them in the plural (early Christian art has shown up to eight, and there is a tradition that suggests twelve was a good 'travelling' number!). Apart from this, Matthew tells us very little about them, presumably because their 'visits' were relatively common at that time and his readership would easily have understand what he meant.

The songs and nativity plays we use at Christmas make a lot of assumptions about these Magi (Source G), much of which has no basis in the Gospels or other contemporary writings. We don't know how many there were, where they came from, or how they travelled. Their names, Gaspar, Melchior and Balthasar, seem to be a third-century invention that neatly reflected the three gifts rather than the number or nature of the people involved. There is no evidence they were kings. They didn't arrive until some time after Jesus' birth, certainly not before all the ritual necessities Jewish Law required were complete (the presentation of Jesus at the temple, his circumcision; and, of course, Mary's forty-day 'purification') by which time, Matthew tells us, they were living in a house. The age of the children massacred by Herod (up to two years old) suggests Jesus may have been a toddler, though probably no older than three, and, as Herod died in 4 BC, the actual year of Jesus' birth is a lot earlier than our calendar would suggest.

Matthew tells us the Magi were observing a bright star before they journeyed to Bethlehem, and again as they arrived. Astronomically, it's likely that this phenomenon was the star Sirius (highly visible in the night sky in the Middle East) in conjunction with the planets Jupiter and Saturn. Taking into account planetary movements and differences in calendars (both then and now), it's likely that Jesus was born in 7 BC, possibly on 17 July. Our use of 25 December began in the fourth century, before which Christians celebrated Jesus' birth on 6 January, the presumed date of his baptism, and the feast of Epiphany.

The meaning of the word Magi has changed over time. It was originally associated with learned Persian advisers who followed the beliefs of Zoroaster, but by the first century it was applied to anyone who was regarded as mysterious in a spiritual way; a person who had access to knowledge that was not usually available to everyone. They were on a quest; were spiritual searchers and scientific researchers; quiet discerners who responded thoughtfully and in a practical way to all they learned. As astronomers and astrologers, they kept track of the movement of time, and were responsible for the workings of the calendar and the tides. They studied medicine and alchemy, and were often employed by rulers and governments as advisers. To them, the journey (in all its senses) was paramount, and they sought neither material nor financial gain from their work; it was shared with all who chose to get involved. They journeyed over great distances in their search for knowledge and understanding, usually in groups, either on foot or on horseback (rather than on camels which were 'beasts of burden' for traders; the equivalent of our HGVs). Their caravans usually travelled at night so they could use the stars for navigation. Daytime travel was usually reserved for roads they knew well.

Matthew tells us they came from the 'east' but does not say precisely where; presumably they were based outside the boundaries of the Roman Empire. As co-ordination of travel was almost impossible at the time, they probably set out from the same place, though they may not have originated from the same racial or spiritual group. Some suggest the Magi were from Mesopotamia (the nearest 'east') where Magi-style learning thrived in the religious freedom that existed before the coming of the Romans. Others suggest they were Persian, Zoroastrians, a view held by the early Church (a mosaic in a basilica in Bethlehem depicts the Magi in Persian dress) and supported by Roman writers. Old Testament scholars suggest Egypt with its strong connections with the use of gold, frankincense and myrrh; or Babylon, with its equally strong tradition of studying the night sky and its role as a centre of learning that was strongly influenced by Jewish thinking.

I. GOLD, FRANKINCENSE AND MYRRH

Gold is familiar to us all as a relatively rare and therefore valuable metal that is used to create special items of jewellery. Back in the days of the 'gold standard', the one-pound bank note, I'm told, could literally be exchanged for a pound weight of gold at the Bank of England. Traditionally, travellers carried gold as a form of currency that was accepted in all parts of the known world. Frankincense and myrrh are less familiar to us. They are both resins made from the dried sap of trees, *Boswellia* (frankincense) and *Commiphora* (myrrh), which are commonly found in the Middle East and North Africa, especially in Ethiopia and Somalia.

Incense (especially frankincense) has always been regarded as sacred and, when burnt, it helps to improve our connection with God and therefore the effectiveness of prayer (as a young chorister I can remember being taught that our prayers 'ascended to God on clouds of incense'). There are many references to its use throughout the Bible, and its healing properties have been used to treat conditions such as catarrh, depression, allergies, headaches, blood pressure, anxiety, coughs, snake bites, sores, TB, diphtheria, meningitis, stress and typhoid.

Myrrh has always been used as incense, to develop spiritual awareness, and as one of the materials used for embalming. It's also been used to treat conditions such as cancer, leprosy, asthma, bronchitis, candida, eczema, piles, ulcers and all kinds of inflammations, as well as a general antiseptic.

Why did the Magi present these three gifts to Jesus and his family? I wonder if these really were gifts in the sense that we understand them. Perhaps the Magi were acknowledging Jesus' future ministry, which would in many ways be a mirror of their own, by sharing the everyday necessities they needed to carry with them. Gold as a means of exchange to provide the basic necessities of life; frankincense and myrrh as important tools for prayer and healing. It's too easy, and inaccurate, to see these as prophetic gifts in the sense of gold for a king, frankincense for a priest and myrrh for suffering and death. They are far more than this, and each, in the way they are used, are both instrumental and symbolic in the transformation of ourselves and others, and the situations we are within. Unless money, prayer and healing are used as instruments of transformation, they are not of any use at all.

J. SAMHAIN* – A CELTIC AUTUMN

Increasing darkness and cold means we must accept that winter is fast approaching and we must adjust to this changing season. Leaves have fallen off the trees, birds have migrated, animals have gone into hibernation, frosts have come. Darkness was important to the Celts. To them it was as important as the light. Darkness and death had power which they did not fear. This dark phase of the year's cycle is when the mystery of transformation occurs. This process involves a death of something old in preparation for something new to be reborn; a journey into the unconscious and the spirit within each of us. We have been taught to fear our inner world and to mistrust the information we may receive through insights, intuition and our connection to our own inherent wisdom. We need to understand our unconscious selves, and to learn to listen to our inner voice. We can use the energy of the dark time of the year to explore these inner parts. Turn and look at what you fear, and the understanding this brings.

The seeds of our ideas and future direction in life are incubated in our unconscious during the winter months, ready for rebirth in the spring. We can honour the cycle by being aware that each end and death of the old will bring an opportunity for a new start as each beginning holds within it an end. This endless cycle of change is necessary, bringing renewal of cells, of ourselves, our understanding and our ideas. It means there are always new opportunities to start again, to stay healthy. Seek the truth in the darkness, look for ways to find the Divine within. Out of a difficult situation comes power, hope, rebirth, inner strength, wisdom and maturity.

*Pronounced 'sow-en'.

Glennie Kindred

K. CELTIC JOURNEYING – ST BRENDAN THE NAVIGATOR

Born in 489 in Tralee, Brendan was brought up on stories of biblical travellers and learned about the mystical Island of Promise over the horizon, a place full of light, fragrant flowers, fruit, and where all the stones were jewels. After consulting with his fellow monks, he fasted for forty days, during which time he saw a vision in which an angel assured him he would see this island. He built a coracle, covering the frame with ox-hides, and set off with fourteen companions. They encountered many islands and experienced hospitable hermits, a fish as large as an island (a whale), an island of sparkling crystal (an iceberg), a barren island with a mountain spitting fire (a volcano), and great swarms of glittering fish. His descriptions tell us he went to the Faroes, Iceland, Greenland and Newfoundland, and possibly North America, the Azores and Spain. He returned enriched, but sad he had not found the Island of Promise after five years. His mother explained that using the skins of animals on the coracle would prevent his landing on the ideal island, for he would spoil its innocence! He set out again, this time in a wooden boat, and discovered the island, which was a place of health, joy, feasting, meadows and angels. But to his great sadness, he was asked to leave before he tainted it. Two years later, he returned home . . . this time a fulfilled person.

Martin Wallace

Shall I abandon, O King of mysteries, the soft comforts of home?
Shall I turn my back on my native land, and my face towards the sea?
Shall I put myself wholly at the mercy of God, without silver,
    without horse, without fame and honour?
Shall I throw myself wholly on the King of kings without sword
    and shield, without food and drink, without a bed to lie on?
Shall I say farewell to my beautiful land, placing myself under
    Christ's yoke?
Shall I pour out my heart to him, confessing my manifold sins, and
    begging forgiveness, tears streaming down my cheeks?
Shall I leave the prints of my knees on the sandy beach, a record of
    my final prayer in my native land?

Shall I then suffer every kind of wound the sea can then inflict?
Shall I take my tiny coracle across the wide, sparkling ocean?
O King of glorious heaven, shall I go of my own choice upon the sea?
O Christ will you help me on the wild waves?

'Brendan's Prayer on the Mountain', by Robert Van de Weyer

L. JOURNEYING

As Dag Hammarskjöld once said, 'The longest journey is the journey inward.' It is here that I need help, and this is one of the reasons why I have found it such a source of strength and inspiration on my own journey to look at the Celtic understanding of *peregrinatio*, a word and concept that is found nowhere else in Christendom. The word itself is almost untranslatable, but its essence is caught in the ninth-century story of three Irishmen drifting over the sea from Ireland for seven days in coracles without oars, coming ashore in Cornwall and then being brought to the court of King Alfred. When he asked them where they had come from and where they were going, they answered that they 'stole away because we wanted for the love of God to be on pilgrimage, we cared not where'. This wonderful response and this amazing undertaking comes out of the inspirational character of early Irish spirituality. It shows at once how misleading is that word 'pilgrimage' and how very different indeed is the Celtic *peregrinatio* from the pilgrimages of the middle ages or the present day. There is no specific end or goal, such as that of reaching a shrine or holy place, which allows the pilgrim at the end of the journey to return home with a sense of mission accomplished. *Peregrinatio* is not undertaken at the suggestion of some monastic abbot or superior but because of an inner prompting in those who set out; a passionate conviction that they must undertake what was essentially an inner journey. Ready to go wherever the Spirit might take them, and seeing themselves as *hospites mundi* – 'guests of the world', what they are seeking is the 'place of their resurrection', the resurrected self, the true self in Christ, which is for all of us our true home . . . However passionate the desire and however total the commitment, this way of *peregrinatio* is bound to be costly.

Esther de Waal

Journeying with the Magi

SESSION 1 – ORIENTATION, MIND CLEARING AND PREPARATION

1. The Welcome

2. Opening Worship (see p. 38)

3. Silence

4. Group or Individual Exploration A

   Using the information in Sources A, B and C discuss the following:
   - What do these accounts tell us of the status of these visitors and their role in their society? (Were there three? Were they men, kings, wise, etc.?)
   - What or who do we feel are their equivalent(s) in today's society, and how do we relate to them as individuals, and as a church?
   - What is their significance for Jesus in this respect?
   - What is their significance for us?
   - In which ways do the accounts agree or disagree with each other?
   - Does it matter?

5. Feedback and Further Discussion from A

6. Silence

7. Other Activity: song (see p. 44 for suggestions), poem, section of video, drama or visual material

8. Group or Individual Exploration B

    Using any relevant points from your earlier discussion, discuss the following:

    - The Magi didn't pop into Tesco's for their 'gifts'. Were these parts of the supplies they normally carried for their journeys, and, if so, what was their significance?
    - What gifts would we give today that are of equal importance?

    Using Sources J, K and L:

    - Reflect on Brendan's preparations for his journeys. What preparations do we need to make for our inner journey through Advent? In which 'direction' should we go? How do we discern which is the right path for us?
    - What do we need to take with us? What do we need to leave behind?

9. Feedback and Further Discussion from B

10. Silence

11. Closing Worship (see p. 40)

SESSION 2 – VALUE: THE GOLD EXPERIENCE

1. The Welcome

2. Relevant Feedback from the Last Session

3. Opening Worship (see p. 38)

4. Silence

5. Group or Individual Exploration A

   Using the relevant sections of Sources G, H and I, discuss the following:
   - What is the traditional view of the significance of gold being given to the infant Jesus?
   - Why did the Magi carry gold?
   - What is its real significance on a spiritual level?

6. Feedback and Further Discussion from A

7. Silence

8. Other Activity: song, poem, section of video, drama or visual material

9. Group or Individual Exploration B

   Using Source D, discuss the following:
   - What do we feel Jesus is teaching about value?
   - What is of most value to us (spiritually, materially, culturally, socially, etc.)?
   - How could this affect the way we use our time and money?
   - How could this affect the way we give generally, and especially at Christmas?

10. Feedback and Further Discussion from B

11. Silence

12. Closing Worship (see p. 40)

SESSION 3 – PRAYER: THE FRANKINCENSE EXPERIENCE

1. The Welcome

2. Relevant Feedback from the Last Session

3. Opening Worship (see p. 38)

4. Silence

5. Group or Individual Exploration A

   Using the relevant sections of Sources G, H and I, discuss the following:
   - What is the traditional view of the significance of frankincense being given to the infant Jesus?
   - Why did the Magi carry frankincense? How and why did they use it? How do we use it today?
   - What is its real significance on a spiritual level?

6. Feedback and Further Discussion from A

7. Silence

8. Other Activity: song, poem, section of video, drama or visual material

9. Group or Individual Exploration B

   Drawing on your own experience and Source E, discuss the following:
   - What is prayer? Why do we pray? How do we pray? What is the purpose of prayer?

- What style of prayer is the most effective for us personally (i.e. the most engaging, or open, or most connecting with God)?
- In which ways do the above extracts give a differing view of prayer as we usually experience it? How significant is the translation from the Aramaic?
- How can we further develop our ways of praying?

10. Feedback and further Discussion from B

11. Silence

12. Closing Worship (see p. 40)

SESSION 4 – HEALING: THE MYRRH EXPERIENCE

1. The Welcome

2. Relevant Feedback from the Last Session

3. Opening Worship (see p. 38)

4. Silence

5. Group or Individual Exploration A

   Using the relevant sections of Sources G, H and I, discuss the following:

   - What is the traditional view of the significance of myrrh being given to the infant Jesus?
   - Why did the Magi carry myrrh? How and why did they use it? How do we use it today?
   - What is its real significance on a spiritual level?

6. Feedback and Further Discussion from A

7. Silence

8. Other Activity: song, poem, section of video, drama or visual material

9. Group or Individual Exploration B

   Drawing on your own experience and Source F, discuss the following:

   - What is healing? Can we all experience it? Can we all be channels for healing or is it a gift for only a few?

- What is the purpose of healing, and at which levels (physical, emotional, mental, spiritual) is it most effective?
- How can we personally broaden the availability of healing?

10. Feedback and Further Discussion from B

11. Silence

12. Closing Worship (see p. 40)

SESSION 5 – THE DAILY EMMAUS EXPERIENCE

I feel strongly that the story of the disciples on the Emmaus road should not be limited to being an appendix of Easter. If we are journeying and truly seeking a daily encounter with Jesus, we need to hold this event and place it within the context of each day and its season. The Emmaus story can be found in Luke, Chapter 24.

1. The Welcome

2. Relevant Feedback from the Last Session

3. Opening Worship (see p. 38)

4. Silence

5. Group or Individual Exploration A

   Using Sources A, B and C, discuss the following:
   - What were the effects of the visit of the Magi for Jesus, Mary and Joseph, the authorities and the local community in a *positive* sense?
   - In a *negative* sense?
   - What were the lessons for the Magi?

6. Feedback and Further Discussion from A

7. Silence

8. Other Activity: song, poem, section of video, drama or visual material

9. Group or Individual Exploration B

Reflect again on the Celtic experience of journeying suggested in Sources J, K and L, and discuss the following:

- What have we personally learned from the Magi for our own journey?

- Reflect for a moment on where you were before you started this course, and identify areas where you feel aspects of the Advent and Christmas season may no longer be appropriate. How would you like to change these this year, and next, at home? At work?

- In our 'church' community – especially what we sing, pray and teach?

- Are there any other aspects of our spiritual journey we would like to change?

- What difficulties might we face taking back our learning, especially in the areas of prayer and healing, and how might we overcome them?

10. Feedback and Further Discussion from B

11. Silence

12. Closing Worship with Communion (see p. 40)

OPENING WORSHIP

Leader 1 It's been a long, long day,
and I've found too little time
to recognise your presence . . .

It's been a long, long day,
and there's been too little quiet
to hear you speak with me . . .

It's been a long, long day,
and I feel too tired
to offer you the best of my abilities . . .

It's been a long, long day,
and I feel a long way
from your love and security . . .

Leader 2 In a time of silence,
let's reflect on how we are at this time . . .
where we are with God . . .
where we are with ourselves . . .
where we are with each other . . .

Let's reflect particularly on this past week . . .
and share with God the times
when we have not
lived up to expectations . . . God's . . . or our own . . .

Let's reflect on the times when we have not
taken opportunities to further the kingdom . . .
when we have not spoken out against injustice . . .
when we have passed by on the other side . . .

Silence

We rest in the stillness of your being.
We rest in the stillness of your love.
We rest in the stillness of your reconciliation
and the knowing that you alone can make us whole.

A song may be sung

CLOSING WORSHIP

Leader 3	Into the love of the Holy Three
All	We place ourselves this night.
Leader 3	Into the care of the Holy Three
All	We place all that we have been, all that we are and all that we shall be.
Leader 3	Into the peace of the Holy Three
All	We place all those things that might trouble or disturb our rest.
Leader 3	This and every night.
All	This and every night.
Leader 3	In the name of the Creator, I ask a blessing of calm on us.
	In the name of the Son, I ask a blessing of peace on us.
	In the name of the Spirit, I ask a blessing of healing on us.
	In the name of the Holy Three, I ask these three blessings on us and those we love today every day each sleep each waking.
All	Amen.

The Blessing

Leader   The peace and love of the Creator be ours;
the peace and love of the Christ be ours;
the peace and love of the Spirit be ours.
As we journey inward during this season of reflection,
may the peace and love of the Holy Three be with us.

All   Amen.

THE PEACE, COMMUNION PRAYER AND BLESSING

The Peace

Leader   As we move and grow
within the rhythms of Samhain/Advent,
may we sense the continuing presence of the Holy Three;
deep peace of the Creator,
gentle love of the Son,
regenerative power of the Spirit.

Let's share a sign of these with each other.

The Communion Prayer

Leader   Come, this is the table,
and this is the sacred meal
blessed and encouraged by Jesus himself.

All are welcome at this table,
however great or small
we feel our faith to be,
or wherever we may be
on our spiritual journey.

As Jesus did,
we bless bread and break it . . .
knowing that, on our spiritual journey,
we need to break those things
that hold us to the past
and challenge the attitudes
that are deeply set within us.

The leader blesses the bread, then each member of the group blesses the bread as it is shared.

Leader   As Jesus did,
we bless wine and share it,
knowing that, on our spiritual journey,
we need to share with love
all we have
and all we are
with the wider community
that is Creation itself.

*The leader blesses the wine, then each member of the
group blesses the wine as it is shared.*

Leader   Be mindful . . .
for to share in this sacred meal
is to commit ourselves to a sacred path
trodden by Christ himself,
and all that it implies
and demands.

The Blessing

Leader   The peace and love of the Creator be ours;
the peace and love of the Christ be ours;
the peace and love of the Spirit be ours.
As we journey inward during this season of reflection,
may the peace and love of the Holy Three be with us.

All   Amen.

SUITABLE SONGS AND RECORDINGS

There are many hymns and songs that reflect both journeying and Advent, and which you may wish to use during this course. I suggest that, after first reading through the course, you can then decide how appropriate these might be, given the nature of this journey.

The following songs (all published either by Kevin Mayhew Publishers or the Iona Community) have accompanied me on my spiritual journeying over the past ten years:

Come, my Lord, my Light, my Way
(from *Sacred Weave*, published by Kevin Mayhew)

Desert waters
(from *Sacred Pathway*, published by Kevin Mayhew)

Evening dedication (from *Sacred Weave*)

Lighten our darkness (from *Sacred Pathway*)

Lord, where have we left you?
(from *Heaven Shall Not Wait*, published by the Iona Community)

Once in Judah's least known city (from *Heaven Shall Not Wait*)

Sing Hey for the Carpenter (from *Heaven Shall Not Wait*)

The Irish blessing (from *Sacred Weave*)

Traveller's prayer (from *Sacred Pathway*)

Travelling the road to freedom (from *Heaven Shall Not Wait*)

When God Almighty came to earth
(from *Heaven Shall Not Wait*)

Will you come and follow me? (from *Heaven Shall Not Wait*)

CDs, cassettes and printed music are available for all the above from The Iona Community (*Heaven Shall Not Wait*) and Kevin Mayhew (*Sacred Weave* and *Sacred Pathway*).

It may also be helpful to have recordings of gentle, reflective music available, preferably instrumental, which will provide an atmosphere before and after the sessions, or maybe help reflection during the silences. There is so much available today on both CD and cassette, but I suggest you listen before you buy to make sure that it provides you with the kind of atmosphere you need.

BIBLIOGRAPHY AND SUGGESTIONS FOR FURTHER READING

Adam, David	*The Edge of Glory – Prayers in the Celtic Tradition* (SPCK, 1985)
Adam, David	*Tides and Seasons – Modern Prayers in the Celtic Tradition* (SPCK, 1989)
Adam, David	*A Desert in the Ocean – God's Call to Adventurous Living* (SPCK, 2000)
Adam, David	*Powerlines – Celtic Prayers about Work* (SPCK, 1992)
De Waal, Esther	*The Celtic Way of Prayer – The Recovery of the Religious Imagination* (Hodder & Stoughton, 1996)
Douglas-Klotz, Neil*	*Prayers of the Cosmos – Meditations on the Aramaic Words of Jesus* (HarperCollins, 1990)†
Douglas-Klotz, Neil	*The Hidden Gospel – Decoding the Spiritual Message of the Aramaic Jesus* (Quest Books, 1999)†
Galloway, Kathy	*A Story to Live By* (SPCK, 1999)
Galloway, Kathy (Ed.)	*Pushing the Boat Out – New Poetry* (Wild Goose Publications, 1995)†
Gilbert, Adrian G.	*Magi – The Quest for a Secret Tradition* (Bloomsbury, 1996)
Hone, William, et al.	*The Lost Books of the Bible* (Testament Books, Random House, 1979)†
Kindred, Glennie	*The Earth's Cycle of Celebration* (Gothic Image Publications, 1991)
Kindred, Glennie	*Sacred Celebrations* (Gothic Image Publications, 2001)†

Mitton, Michael	*Restoring the Woven Cord* (Darton, Longman & Todd, 1995)†
Murray Schafer, R.	*Ear Cleaning: Notes for An Experimental Music Course* (Universal Edition, 1967)
Seymour, P. A. H.	*The Birth of Christ – Exploding the Myth* (Virgin, 1999)†
Van de Weyer, Robert	*Celtic Fire* (Darton, Longman & Todd, 1990)
Wallace, Martin	*A Celtic Resource Book* (National Society/Church House Publishing, 1998)†

Searching the Internet can also be fascinating. There are many, many sites that discuss the Magi (for example), some totally fanciful, some frighteningly fundamentalist, and some very creative in their thinking!

* Although Neil Douglas-Klotz is particularly well known as a linguist and scholar of Middle Eastern languages, all his work is deeply spiritual and embodies a journey to unravel the authentic voice and teachings of Jesus by researching and meditating upon the Aramaic that Jesus spoke. His main source is the Syriac Aramaic manuscript of the Gospels, also known as the Peshitta version, thought to date from the second century. Aramaic was the everyday language spoken by the 'person in the street' (as well as by Jesus and the disciples) and, along with Hebrew and Arabic, can express a number of different layers of meaning within a single word or phrase. For example, the word *sema* may be translated as 'name', 'light', 'sound' or 'experience'. The mystical tradition suggests we should consider all viewpoints and interpretations of the sayings of Jesus and hold them to work inside ourselves; this becomes much more effective if we also hold the differing Aramaic levels of meaning at the literal, metaphoric and mystical levels. For a more detailed explanation, see Neil's book *Prayers of the Cosmos*, which also contains a summary of his work with the Aramaic versions of the Lord's Prayer and the Beatitudes.

† Indicates books that have been used as the principal sources for this course. All the books listed, however, are relevant to the wider issues of journeying and the Celtic way. My versions of the extracts from the Gospels of James and Joseph the Priest are based on material from William Hone's *The Lost Books of the Bible*.